PRAISE

A WEAPON
OF WARFARE
& DELIVERANCE

D1554654

FRANK HAMMOND

PRAISE:
A WEAPON OF WARFARE AND DELIVERANCE

BY FRANK HAMMOND

ISBN 10: 0-89228-385-8
ISBN 13: 978-089228-385-9

IMPACT CHRISTIAN BOOKS, INC.
332 Leffingwell Ave., Suite 101
Kirkwood, MO 63122

WWW.IMPACTCHRISTIANBOOKS.COM

PRAISE:
A WEAPON OF WARFARE AND DELIVERANCE

INTRODUCTION

Praise is a weapon of spiritual warfare. As you praise the Lord, powerful things begin to happen in the heavenly realm. Paul tells us in 2 Corinthians 10:4 that:

> **For the weapons of our warfare are not carnal, but mighty through God to the pulling down of strong holds**

God has given us, as believers, spiritual weapons. This passage reminds us of the weapons, and the power that is in those weapons.

There are several important things that are said in this verse about the spiritual weapons that God gives into the hands of his spiritual army. First of all, he says that the weapons are non-carnal. That means they are not of the flesh. The reason we cannot use fleshly weapons in our warfare is because our enemy is not fleshly; he is a spiritual enemy. So it takes spiritual weapons to defeat spiritual enemies. No kind of physical or fleshly weapon is effective in deliverance and spiritual warfare. You cannot shoot your enemies with a gun, you cannot cut them with a sword, you cannot drop a bomb on them. There are other kinds of fleshly weapons that people try to use against evil spirits, like education. Some people think if they are smart enough, or educated enough, evil spirits will not bother them. So, for them, man's education is a weapon of warfare. Yet, Paul says here you cannot use fleshly weapons, but you can use spiritual weapons and these are "mighty through God."

These weapons seem to be foolish to the carnal mind, but they are entirely successful! They cannot know failure. The weapons that God puts in our hands are completely effective for the warfare that we have before us.

Paul says they are mighty in God through "the pulling down of strong holds." Now, when someone has a strong hold, that means that they have set up a fortress, and they are established in that place. Paul is saying these weapons can be used to pull down strong holds or fortresses that the enemy has set up in our lives and the lives of others.

The devil says to us, "I am entrenched!" So what? The weapons that we have are effective in precisely this kind of situation. When the devil has done his best to secure himself in a position, he is still vulnerable. He is still defeatable.

HATRED FOR GOD'S WEAPONS

Every one of the weapons that God has given us is hated, despised and ridiculed.

Take the blood of Jesus for instance; there are a lot of people who ridicule the blood of Jesus. There have been quite a few people of "modern theology" who have called the blood sacrifice of Jesus a *slaughterhouse* religion. They say it is not necessary to talk about the blood, and the blood of Jesus is not important. That is an effort to take this weapon away from you. Do you see that? A lot of churches don't sing about the blood, don't preach about the blood, don't testify about the blood. As a result, they lose their power and influence because they disregard their spiritual weaponry.

The same thing has been done concerning the name of Jesus. The name of Jesus is a powerful weapon! The apostles were forbidden by the magistrates from speaking in the name of Jesus. Who was behind that effort to take the name of Jesus out of the witness of the early disciples? The person behind this also makes Christians today timid and fearful of talking about their precious Lord Jesus. Who would want to make us timid? Who would want to make us afraid? Who would want to take that name out of our mouths? The one who knows the power that is in that name! Satan, of course.

There are other weapons that God has given to us. The Word of God is a weapon. The Bible says that it is like a two-edged sword. We are to take up the sword of the Spirit which is the word of God. Do you know that the devil would rather have us quote any other book than the Word of God? You can quote Shakespeare and Keats all day long and it does not bother him one bit. When you start quoting the Word of God, he trembles. He falls into fear.

THE WEAPON OF PRAISE

Then there is praise. Praise is a mighty weapon and the enemy is fearful of it. He detests it because he fears it. And why does he fear it? Because it is such a powerful weapon against him.

There are a lot of people who say that they are Christians but they hate genuine praise. We have had people come into our church while we were worshiping and do a U-turn and walk right out. Others have stuck it out, but have been miserable during the whole time of praise.

Who is it that makes people afraid of genuine praise? Who is it that makes them uncomfortable? The Word of God says that we are to praise the Lord! Who is it that tries to keep mouths shut, tries to keep the voices in a whisper? To be sure, it's not the power of God's Holy Spirit. Praise is a weapon against the power of the devil and the devil does everything that he can to stop one from moving into praise.

Some churches fear genuine praise. They are afraid that it will run off the prospective members. They want to tone down what God is stirring up! We have decided in our church that we are not going to adjust to the world or to those who are timid and afraid but, rather, they are going to have to adjust to God's Word.

Hallelujah! Don't ever be afraid of the praise that goes up from your heart. There may be people who laugh at you or try to ridicule you. But I say "I am a fool for Jesus, who are you a fool for?"

STRANGE WEAPONS

Have you ever thought about the strange weapons and tactics that are deployed in warfare in Scripture? Think about Samson who used a weapon one day in the form of a jawbone of an ass. With this jawbone he killed 1,000 Philistines! Now that was a powerful weapon but it certainly was a strange one, wasn't it?

Then there was the judge named Shangar. He took an ox goad, the thing you use to prod the ox to make them go, and with this strange weapon he slaughtered 600 of the enemy.

And then there was Gideon, the one God called to go against a mighty host, and God said "You have too many." God said to eliminate most of those who had volunteered. The army was reduced to 300 men, and only they would come against a mighty army, a great host. Do you know what the weapons were that day? A water pitcher with a torch inside of it, and a trumpet! With those strange tools a vast army was defeated.

There were others who had strange weapons. Think about David when he was confronted with Goliath. With King Saul and all of his army, yet all the men still were afraid of Goliath. But David knew the Lord. He took a slingshot and a few smooth stones and slayed the giant. Praise the Lord! The power of God's weaponry is awesome.

When Joshua led the children of Israel against the city of Jericho, they marched, and at the sound of a signal, they shouted. They blew a few ram horns. With this, the walls of the city came down, and a great victory was won by the Lord that day.

God has chosen throughout his Word to use some strange weapons and tactics to gain victory. It should not be any surprise that this is true of some of the weapons He has given us: the name of Jesus, the blood of Jesus, the word of our testimony, the Word of God, praise, prayer — all are unexpected, but powerful, weapons. Just as these strange weapons God used in the Old Testament were powerful, the ones that God has given to us today are powerful, and more so!

PSALM 149
A PSALM OF PRAISE WARFARE

This is a Psalm of warfare, and praise is the weaponry that is employed. I would like to explore some of the details included in this passage. This Psalm starts by saying,

Praise ye the Lord. Sing unto the Lord a new song, and his praise in the congregation of saints.

The word "praise" here is one of about six different words used for praise in the Old Testament. It is the Hebrew word *halel* from which we get our English word *hallelujah*. Literally interpreted, *halel* means "to make a show," as in the opposite of being pious. That is what God uses for the word for praise: be *halel!*

Think about how people act in a football stadium or at a baseball game. See what kind of celebratory displays are shown when a team scores or makes an important play. Why there, and not in the house of God? Let's get excited about what our great God has done for us!

We should find something to get excited about in all the blessings, tremendous salvations, and outpourings of God's grace and mercy. We should find something to get excited about when we think of God's deliverance and His power over the enemy.

PRAISE IS AN
OVERFLOW OF GRATITUDE

Praise is the overflow of our heart in gratitude for God's goodness to us. If you are happy about what God has done for you, you will not sit in your chair like a bump on a log. If you truly are grateful for what God has done in your life, and you appreciate it and are thankful for it, then there is a well that starts flowing out of you, bubbling up inside of you, and it's going to overflow in praise.

In the first verse of Psalm 149 he says:

...sing to the Lord...

There is a time to sing *about the Lord*, and Scripture also says there is a time to sing *to the Lord*. I'm glad so many of the songs God has given us today are sung to the Lord. We are singing directly to Jesus. He is a person, He's real, and He's listening. He takes pleasure in our praise and our singing. So we sing to the Lord and sometimes we sing a new song to the Lord.

The Spirit once showed me something interesting about singing *new songs* to the Lord. These are songs that are probably sung just one time by you, never published, never repeated, just sung one time. If you have not done this, try it.

PRAISE IS CATALYST
TO THE SPIRIT MOVING

Have you ever noticed how many of the prophecies, tongues, interpretations, visions, and other ministries of the Holy Spirit come after we have been praising the Lord? There is a reason for that. When we praise the Lord we are ministering to the Lord. Praise is our ministry to the Lord. When we minister to the Lord, He inhabits our praise, and as His presence and power begin to envelop us, He then ministers to us! We minister to Him and He reciprocates. He returns the blessing.

> **Praise ye the Lord. Sing unto the Lord a new song, and his praise in the congregation of saints.**

So we are to praise God in the assembly or "congregation" of the saints. In Psalm 68:4, in the AMPLIFIED BIBLE (AMPC), it says:

> **...sing praises to His name, cast up a highway for Him**

Isn't that a beautiful expression? When we have praised the Lord, we have thrown up a highway. We have provided a way of entrance for the Lord to come into our midst. He rides on the praises of his people, as if He is traveling on a highway directly to us!

SOMETIMES WE STRUGGLE TO ENTER INTO PRAISE

Sometimes you come into the presence of the Lord in a church and you are not in a good enough mood to praise the Lord. How many of us have been in that situation? I think all of us have had times like that. Turn to James 5:13. James is talking about when the Church comes together and what it ought to do:

Is any among you afflicted?

The literal translation of afflicted is *ill-treated.* Are any of you ill-treated? Before you left home, perhaps your husband barked at you, or somebody stepped on your toes and offended you. That is what the word afflicted means! When you come into the service feeling afflicted, you are spiritually crippled. Your feet won't dance and your hands won't go up. You're afflicted.

James tells you what to do about it.

Let him pray.

What should an afflicted person pray about? He is going to pray until he gets all of the unforgiveness out of his heart. He is going to pray until his heart is healed from that affliction. He's going to pray until he feels free again!

Is any of you happy? Let him sing songs.

He says that when you're happy, come in to church singing praises to God. That is going to help the ones who are praying through affliction.

You see, the objective is for us to come together as the *army of the Lord.* If half of the troops are on sick-call, it's not much of an army. If half of them are afflicted and they cannot get their heart into the battle, or into the flow of God's Spirit, the whole service can be sick. So, he says, let's find a way through it and get the team together and the army into unity. Let's get things to flow!

When we are afflicted, Scripture says that we have a responsibility before God to do something about it. If you are afflicted and you do nothing about it, you can put a damper on the service. God says to get on your knees and pray, make things right and get your heart settled. Get in tune with the Lord. Stabilize in His love.

The ones that come in happy, let them start praising the Lord and that will lift the others. And then he says,

Are any of you sick?

Where's the best place to be when you're sick? The church. He says if you are sick or have pain in your body,

> Let him call for the elders of the church; and let them pray over him, anointing him with oil in the name of the Lord: And the prayer of faith shall save the sick, and the Lord shall raise him up...

And,

> **if he have committed sins, they shall be forgiven him.**

We have, until now, been ministering to the sick at the end of the service. God is telling us to do it at the beginning of the service. Then, when all the afflicted and lame are touched by the Lord, everyone is able to focus and praise in unity, and use praise as a weapon.

Praise is a spiritual force against the power of the enemy. The devil will do everything he can to keep us defeated; to keep us from rising up and singing and dancing before the Lord. That ought to make us mad. If there is anything that should make a Christian fighting mad, that is it! You say back to him:

> **"Devil how dare you! You are not going to put that stuff on me, I'm not going to have the spirit of heaviness, I am going to have the garments of praise. Glory to Jesus!"**

PRAISE BRINGS TRIUMPH OVER DEMONIC SPIRITS

Continuing in Psalm 149, it says:

Let Israel rejoice in him that made him: let the children of Zion be joyful in their King.

The word that is translated *rejoice* is a Hebrew word that is also translated *triumph*. This is another common word for praise in the Old Testament. "Let the children of Zion triumph!" He is talking about being triumphant through the act of praise. In other words, there is a type of praise that puts the enemy to flight and defeats the devil. *Hallelujah!* When you start praising, you begin triumphing.

Think about it. In the Old Testament, they didn't have the blood of Jesus as a weapon; they didn't have the name of Jesus as a weapon, but *they did have* praise. Recall when Saul was troubled by an evil spirit. The only way they knew to help him was to have David play on a harp and sing praise in the king's presence. What did it say happened when David began to play on his harp and sing praise to God? The evil spirit departed from King Saul!

You can see why praise was so important to the Old Testament saints. You can see why they developed such a lifestyle of praise.

VARIOUS WAYS
TO EXPRESS PRAISE

Going on in Psalm 149, it says in verse three:

Let them praise his name in the dance: let them sing praises unto him with the timbrel and harp.

Here the psalmist begins to describe the various ways that praise can be expressed. One of the ways is by singing, whether by groups or by individuals. Another way is through dance. The word here for *dance* can mean either an individual or a group dance. The Hebrew word for dance here literally means *to twist* or *to turn*. Another Hebrew word for dance means to "move nimbly." And still another Hebrew word for dance means "to leap" and "to skip."

I have seen meetings where people begin to dance during worship in the Spirit and it looked like they were floating on air, light and feathery. That is dancing unto the Lord. It is not a *fleshly* form of dancing, or a dancing to try to *draw attention to oneself*, it is the dancing that comes from emptying oneself.

Then he names various instruments you can perform praise on. If you follow on to Psalm 150, he talks more about the instruments.

And then in verse five of Psalm 149, he says:

Let the saints be joyful in glory: let them sing aloud upon their beds.

After you get through singing praises in church, you go home and you are still praising God! You were praising God standing up, now you are praising God laying down. You praise him in the daytime and you praise him in the nighttime. In every circumstance and every situation, even upon your beds.

THE HIGH PRAISES OF GOD

Psalm 149 continues on to say:

Let the high praises of God be in their mouth, and a two-edged sword in their hand;

This is the only time in the whole of Scripture that the term "high praises of God" is used. It means to "exalt God, to glorify God, to magnify God out of your heart." The high praises of God signifies praise that comes from deep within us, running out of our hearts. It is the expression of exultation, magnification, and glorification of God. Those are the high praises of God.

It's not about how loud you sing, how active you get, but it is from how deep inside of you that praise comes when it reaches the surface. Let your praise come out of a heart in deep gratitude, thanksgiving, and love for the Lord. Let it come up as an expression of praise unto him — the high praises of God. It begins in your heart, but it has to get into your mouth for it to become praise. It has to be vocalized and expressed. In order for it to become praise, it must be expressed.

A "two edged sword in your hand" refers to the Word of God. The Word of God and praise are common companions, and are closely related.

TO PUNISH
AND TORMENT DEMONS

In verse seven of Psalm 149, he says we praise God in order to...

To execute vengeance upon the heathen, and punishments upon the people...

This has a spiritual meaning to it. He is talking here about the Satanic nations, the principalities and powers of the devil. The devil has nations of demons set up in the heavenly realm. The Psalmist says we are going to reap vengeance upon these nations through our praise, and execute punishment on the peoples.

Do you realize that demons are punished and tormented by praise? I want you to understand what your praise does in the spirit realm! A demon cannot exist in that environment. He cannot function in that environment. It would be like a fish trying to exist out of water, or a human trying to exist where there is no air. You simply cannot function in that environment. So when we get into the praise of God we are creating an environment in which the devil cannot function! Think of young David praising before King Saul. The demons cannot move; they cannot do their work in that atmosphere. Are you beginning to see how important it is for us to praise the Lord?

Demons have tormented us enough, and through praise we get to turn the tables, and *torment them*. That sounds like a good thing to me.

PRAISE IS PART OF GOD'S GOVERNMENTAL AUTHORITY

In verse eight of Psalm 149, he says,

> To bind their kings with chains, and their nobles with fetters of iron…

That word bind means to "keep in prison" or "to restrain by governmental authority or command." When you bind these spiritual potentates, these kings and nobles, you are imprisoning them and immobilizing them by governmental authority. Now what government is he talking about? The Kingdom of God. We represent the Kingdom of God, and we function in the authority of God's Kingdom. So we have the power through our commands backed by governmental authority to bind the demonic nobles and the kings with chains and fetters of iron. *Hallelujah!*

> To execute upon them the judgment written: this honour have all his saints. Praise ye the Lord.

"This honour have *all* the saints" means that this is something every believer can do. You can defeat the enemy with the weapon of praise. Everyone of us can do it, with no exceptions.

JEHOSHAPHAT GOES INTO
BATTLE WITH PRAISE

Now let's turn to 2 Chronicles, where we see a live demonstration of the weapon of praise in action. I will walk you through the story of Jehoshaphat and how he set up a choir that sang and overcame the enemy.

We begin in Chapter 18, where we learn that Jehoshaphat messed some things up. He decided that he would be in league with the king of Israel, the evil King Ahab, and through this he was almost killed. As he was coming back from that battle, still licking his wounds, God's prophet met him and said, essentially, "Brother, you just about did it. You almost died."

Then in the next chapter, 2 Chronicles 19, we see that Jehoshaphat is laying a strong spiritual foundation for himself and for the people of Judah. In verse three, the prophet says to him:

Nevertheless there are good things found in thee, in that thou hast taken away the groves out of the land, and hast prepared thine heart to seek God.

Jehoshaphat "took the groves out of the land." What does this mean? It means that he removed idolatry from the land of Judah. This is one of the good things that he had in his favor, that he had removed idolatry out of the land.

And then it says "thou… hast prepared thine heart to seek the Lord God." Because he had removed the idols, his heart and the nation's heart was no longer divided, so he had prepared himself to properly seek the Lord. Now that is important to what happens in Chapter 20, and it is important to what happens from now on in our lives as well. It is important that we remove everything foreign to God out of our lives, any idolatrous thing, and to prepare ourselves to seek the Lord.

Then in 2 Chronicles 19:5, Jehoshaphat appointed some judges to be rulers and magistrates in the land. Look what King Jehoshaphat said to these judges:

> **Wherefore now let the fear of the Lord be upon you; take heed and do it: for there is no iniquity with the Lord our God, nor respect of persons, nor taking of gifts** *[i.e., bribes]*.

He said, in essence, to those judges:

> **"I charge you, as you fulfill your responsibilities, you fear the Lord. You do a job of justice and equity and fairness. Don't take bribes, and don't you mistreat anybody."**

This is still part of the foundation that Jehoshaphat is laying for what comes next in Chapter 20. In verse nine, he saw to it that the ministry of the priest was reestablished, and this is what he said to the priests:

And he charged them, saying, Thus shall ye do in the fear of the Lord, faithfully, and with a perfect heart.

He said, in essence, to the priests,

"When you minister before the Lord in the tabernacle, you be sure that you're doing it in fear or respect of the Lord. You be sure that your ministry to God is faithful and done with a right heart before the Lord."

What we're seeing is that Jehoshaphat instituted spiritual reforms in the nation, and as a result, the people were living lives that were pleasing to the Lord, having turned their hearts completely to God.

Now let's move into chapter 20.

It came to pass after this also, that the children of Moab, and the children of Ammon, and with them other beside the Ammonites, came against Jehoshaphat to battle.

Then there came some that told Jehoshaphat, saying, There cometh a great multitude against thee from beyond the sea on this side Syria; and, behold, they be in Hazazontamar, which is Engedi.

So Jehoshaphat the King received this message, a dire warning, and was asked "What are you going to do? Our enemies are on the borders of our nation! There's a whole horde of warriors and chariots and armed men coming to invade us!"

In verse three we are told Jehoshaphat feared:

> **And Jehoshaphat feared, and set himself to seek the Lord, and proclaimed a fast throughout all Judah.**
>
> 2 Chron. 20:3

This reminds me of what the psalmist says: "At what time I am afraid I will trust in God." The fear that Jehoshaphat experienced caused him to seek God. Then he began to pray and fast and call upon God.

> **And Judah gathered themselves together, to ask help of the Lord: even out of all the cities of Judah they came to seek the Lord.**
>
> 2 Chron. 20:4

You can see the attitude of the people. They did not panic. They were following their leader, Jehoshaphat, who was praying and fasting, and the people fell right into step and began to seek the Lord too. From all the cities of Judah they came to seek the Lord.

Next, he testifies of the greatness and the power of God.

And Jehoshaphat stood in the congregation of Judah and Jerusalem, in the house of the Lord, before the new court,

And said, O Lord God of our fathers, art not thou God in heaven? and rulest not thou over all the kingdoms of the heathen? and in thine hand is there not power and might, so that none is able to withstand thee?

2 Chron. 20:5–6

This is the confession that is coming out of his mouth. He began to proclaim the greatness of God. He was speaking words of faith, and confessing his recognition of the power of God to help. This is what we are supposed to do, too. God already knows what our problem is, before we even tell him.

Art not thou our God, who didst drive out the inhabitants of this land before thy people Israel, and gavest it to the seed of Abraham thy friend for ever?

2 Chron. 20:7

Jehoshaphat is saying: "You are the Lord that has already rescued Your people. You have already brought us into our inheritance."

They had moved into their inheritance, but the enemy was plotting. You cannot let your guard down, or let your defenses down, you have to stay in the ways of God. You must avoid passivity in your spiritual life.[1] Just because you have had victories with the Lord, and you are walking with the Lord today, doesn't mean that the devil chooses to forget about you the rest of your life. We see here that Satan had not forgotten about Israel. He was plotting destruction for them, or at the very least, trying to hinder God's people.

> **If, when evil cometh upon us, as the sword, judgment, or pestilence, or famine, we stand before this house, and in thy presence, (for thy name is in this house,) and cry unto thee in our affliction, then thou wilt hear and help.**
>
> 2 Chron. 20:9

He said here that it doesn't matter if it's war they were facing, or judgment, or pestilence, or famine. The Lord had said that if His people were to stand before His house and invoke His name and call on Him, God would come to their rescue. And this holds true for us today.

---

1 See *The Perils of Passivity*, by Frank Hammond, Impact Christian Books.

> And now, behold, the children of Ammon and
> Moab and mount Seir, whom thou wouldest
> not let Israel invade, when they came out of the
> land of Egypt, but they turned from them, and
> destroyed them not;
>
> Behold, I say, how they reward us, to come to
> cast us out of thy possession, which thou hast
> given us to inherit.
>
> 2 Chron. 20:10–11

Notice how the enemy really tries to get us out of our inheritance, which is the Kingdom of God. When we are in the Kingdom, we are in righteousness, peace, and joy in the Holy Spirit. We are content, we are at peace, we are at rest. But when the devil sees us as such, it drives him crazy. So he devises plans and strategies to try to get us out of our inheritance, so that we lose the closeness to God's Spirit and fall short on the fruit of the Spirit in our lives.

> O our God, wilt thou not judge them? for we
> have no might against this great company that
> cometh against us; neither know we what to
> do: but our eyes are upon thee.
>
> 2 Chron. 20:12

Our own strength, our own flesh, our own resources are totally insufficient and ineffective in spiritual warfare. This is what Jehoshaphat is telling us here. So, we instead turn our eyes to the Lord. Judah was not turning to Egypt to the South or to Israel to the North, as they had done in times past; they were strictly relying on the Lord. This is a major change in heart for them.

> And all Judah stood before the Lord, with their little ones, their wives, and their children.
>
> Then upon Jahaziel the son of Zechariah, the son of Benaiah, the son of Jeiel, the son of Mattaniah, a Levite of the sons of Asaph, came the Spirit of the Lord in the midst of the congregation…
>
> 2 Chron. 20:14

The Spirit of God moved in the midst of that congregation, and moved upon Jahaziel, a son of Asaph. His family was responsible for gathering and recording all the songs of praise.

God's Spirit moved upon Jahaziel and he began to prophesy. Take a moment and listen to the prophecy that came out:

> And he said, Hearken ye, all Judah, and ye inhabitants of Jerusalem, and thou king Jehoshaphat, Thus saith the Lord unto you, Be not afraid nor dismayed by reason of this great multitude; for the battle is not yours, but God's.

Tomorrow go ye down against them: behold, they come up by the cliff of Ziz; and ye shall find them at the end of the brook, before the wilderness of Jeruel.

2 Chron. 20:15–16

Pay careful attention to what is in operation here. Did you catch it? It is a *gift of knowledge*,[2] where the Lord is telling the nation of Judah where the enemy is going to be and how to cut him off at the pass. *Hallelujah!*

Ye shall not need to fight in this battle: set yourselves, stand ye still, and see the salvation of the Lord with you, O Judah and Jerusalem: fear not, nor be dismayed; tomorrow go out against them: for the Lord will be with you.

2 Chron. 20:17

The Lord was telling them that they had to stand in faith. If fear came in they could not stand in faith. God said to them "Don't be dismayed, don't be fearful, don't be hopeless. Tomorrow go out against them because the Lord will be with you!"

---

2 Refer to this gift in the New Testament, found in 1 Corinthians 12:8.

When Jehoshaphat heard this, he...

> ...bowed his head with his face to the ground:
> and all Judah and the inhabitants of Jerusalem
> fell before the Lord, worshipping the Lord.
>
> 2 Chron. 20:18

Notice their response to this prophecy was *worship*. This continues in the next verse:

> And the Levites, of the children of the Kohathites,
> and of the children of the Korhites, stood up to
> praise the Lord God of Israel with a loud voice
> on high.

The people of God stood up and began to praise with a loud voice. Remember, we have not even come to the battle yet! This is the foundation that was being laid, the spiritual foundation. They were doing their homework, and they did it through praise.

> And they rose early in the morning, and went forth
> into the wilderness of Tekoa: and as they went
> forth, Jehoshaphat stood and said, Hear me, O
> Judah, and ye inhabitants of Jerusalem; Believe
> in the Lord your God, so shall ye be established;
> believe his prophets, so shall ye prosper.
>
> 2 Chron. 20:20

Jehoshaphat is saying that they will not take the enemy in victory if they do not go out in faith. "Believe the prophets," he exhorts, and the people "will prosper." God had spoken through His prophets — now it was the people's turn to trust and believe in the Lord. The prophets in the Old Testament only spoke the Word of God. When you read books like Isaiah and Jeremiah and the rest of the prophets, you are reading the prophet's words, which *are the Word of God*. So Jehoshaphat is essentially saying to Judah, and to us today, "have faith in the Word of God, have faith in His promises!"

God had made a promise to go with them, deliver them out of the hand of the enemy, and give them victory. God is saying the same thing to me and to you through the words of Jehoshaphat. We are not going to have victory, like we want, unless we stand.

> **Wherefore take unto you the whole armour of God, that ye may be able to withstand in the evil day, and having done all, to stand.**
>
> **Eph. 6:13**

Unless we trust in God and His promises, we will not have the fullness of victory that we desire.

> **And when he had consulted with the people, he appointed singers unto the Lord, and that should praise the beauty of holiness, as they**

> went out before the army, and to say, Praise
> the Lord; for his mercy endureth for ever.
>
> 2 Chron. 20:21

He sent a choir to go before the armed troops, to sing praises to the Lord, "for His mercy endureth forever." Just a simple praise they were to sing; isn't that powerful? Surely it had to sound ridiculous to the enemies who heard them coming.

> And when they began to sing and to praise, the Lord set ambushments against the children of Ammon, Moab, and mount Seir, which were come against Judah; and they were smitten.
>
> For the children of Ammon and Moab stood up against the inhabitants of mount Seir, utterly to slay and destroy them: and when they had made an end of the inhabitants of Seir, every one helped to destroy another.

The word for that is *confusion*. This is a powerful example of what happens in the heavenly realm when you begin to praise the Lord — it causes confusion in the camp of the enemy. Saints, the demons go nuts! They go into confusion, they begin to attack one another.

PRAISE CAUSES CONFUSION IN
THE CAMP OF THE ENEMY

Let me give you a few parallel passages on that point.
Look at Psalm 35:26–27:

> Let them be ashamed and brought to confusion
> together that rejoice at mine hurt: let them be
> clothed with shame and dishonour that magnify
> themselves against me.

> Let them shout for joy, and be glad, that
> favour my righteous cause: yea, let them say
> continually, Let the Lord be magnified, which
> hath pleasure in the prosperity of his servant.

David is saying to us "OK, the devil is moving in but he
is going to be confounded. He is going to be ashamed. He
is going to be brought into confusion and everyone who is
on my side should start praising the Lord with me."

In Psalm 70, we see the same promise again:

> Let them be ashamed and confounded that seek
> after my soul: let them be turned backward, and
> put to confusion, that desire my hurt.

> Let them be turned back for a reward of their
> shame that say, Aha, aha.

Let all those that seek thee rejoice and be glad in thee: and let such as love thy salvation say continually, Let God be magnified.

Psalm 70:2–4

David brought the enemy into confusion through the praise of God's people.

Also look at Psalm 109:

Let mine adversaries be clothed with shame, and let them cover themselves with their own confusion, as with a mantle.

I will greatly praise the Lord with my mouth; yea, I will praise him among the multitude.

Psalm 109:29–30

Praise God! The praises of the people of God have caused the adversary to be clothed in shame and covered with confusion. Praising God not only follows the confusion and defeat of the enemy; it *precedes* the confusion and defeat of the enemy. Praise is a powerful weapon against the power of the devil.

BINDING THE STRONGMAN
AND TAKING HIS TREASURES (SPOIL)

Returning to 2 Chronicles 20:

And when Judah came toward the watch tower in the wilderness, they looked unto the multitude, and, behold, they were dead bodies fallen to the earth, and none escaped.

And when Jehoshaphat and his people came to take away the spoil of them, they found among them in abundance both riches with the dead bodies, and precious jewels, which they stripped off for themselves, more than they could carry away: and they were three days in gathering of the spoil, it was so much.

2 Chron. 20:24–25

Praising the Lord had bound and defeated the enemy, and the people of God went in and spoiled his house! First you bind the enemy, in this case through praise, and then you spoil his house (Matt. 12:29, Mark 3:27).[3] They went in to the camp of the enemy and took spoil. In the same way, the devil today has a lot of precious things that belong to the people of God. When we defeat those "kings," we too will spoil their houses and we'll take away precious jewels and gems that the devil is holding in his snare. We will spoil his house!

3 Refer to the Audio Teaching *Spoiling the Enemy's House* (CD) by Frank Hammond, Impact Christian Books

This reminds me of the powerful promise for deliverance written into the prophecy of Cyrus in Isaiah 45:

> "I will go before you and make the rough places smooth; I will shatter the doors of bronze and cut through their iron bars. I will give you the treasures of darkness and hidden wealth of secret places, So that you may know that it is I, The Lord, the God of Israel, who calls you by your name.
>
> Isaiah 45:2–3 (NASB)

God "breaks through gates of bronze" and "cuts through bars of iron" to deliver His people from the snares of Satan. But He does not stop there. He has a purpose in this victory and that is to reveal the "treasures of darkness, riches stored in secret places" within you. You see, God sees the gold hidden inside you, and He wants to vanquish the enemy so that your treasure can be brought into the light, and can be used to its fullest potential.

> And on the fourth day they assembled themselves in the valley of Berachah; for there they blessed the Lord: therefore the name of the same place was called, the valley of Berachah, unto this day.
>
> 2 Chron. 20:26

They praised before the battle, they praised during the battle, and then, after the victory, they praised again after the battle! This was the lifestyle of the people in the Old Testament who had victory. They had their lives in order; their priorities were in order. They had removed the garbage out of their lives (2 Chron. 19), and they were seeking the Lord. They were living in justice. They were serving God and worshiping Him with sincere hearts.

So when the day of battle finally came and they went out to meet their enemy (2 Chron. 20), they were already versed in praise, because this was their lifestyle, their daily practice. They were prepared. It was nothing new to them when God told them to go before the enemy and use praise as a form of warfare.

> **Then they returned, every man of Judah and Jerusalem, and Jehoshaphat in the forefront of them, to go again to Jerusalem with joy; for the Lord had made them to rejoice over their enemies.**
>
> **And they came to Jerusalem with psalteries and harps and trumpets unto the house of the Lord.**
>
> **And the fear of God was on all the kingdoms of those countries, when they had heard that the Lord fought against the enemies of Israel.**
>
> **2 Chron. 20:27–29**

Notice, this was not just one victory, *but many victories* wrapped into one. Judah's triumph put fear in the hearts of all the kingdoms who learned of this victory. All their neighbors heard that the Lord God fights for Israel. You can see the level of defeat their enemy experienced. It not only defeated the enemy coming against them, but it curtailed any designs against Judah by the rest of the surrounding kingdoms. Think about the implications of this for our own spiritual lives.

Saints, consider the power of praise. We are seeing what God by his Spirit is doing in the heavenly realm for us. We are seeing what is being accomplished through our praise in God. Our praise to the Lord is essential and vital. It's so important.

> **So the realm of Jehoshaphat was quiet: for his God gave him rest round about.**
> 2 Chron. 20:30

Jehoshaphat's enemy had been defeated. As a result, his whole kingdom was at peace. His whole kingdom was at rest. Do you see the level of victory God has in store for you? And the weapon that brought the victory was praise.

Oh, that we would appreciate the power of praise! With Jehoshaphat, God has given us insight into what praise truly produces in the spiritual realm. Let us take this lesson to heart so that we might develop and maintain a lifestyle of praise. I am talking about genuine and sincere praise, to the point of even praising God on our bed.

I'm not talking about a "put on," or something worked up in the flesh. I am talking about something that flows out of the innermost part of us. I am talking about being so full of what God means to you and His goodness to you that there is no lid big enough or strong enough to hold that fountain of praise back. It is going to gush out like an artesian well.

CONCLUSION

We must not, under any circumstance, let the enemy rob us of our weapons; he cannot be allowed to take our weapons away from us. I don't care what others say, what wisecracks they make about us because we praise the Lord and dance, shout and sing. Don't become afraid or become timid. Don't become embarrassed. The devil can use shame and embarrassment to take a weapon away from you that is of tremendous power against him and his demons.

Praise is one of the powerful, spiritual weapons we have been given. We need to use it effectively, and in a timely way, against all the powers of wickedness.

Amen!

FRANK HAMMOND BOOKS & E-BOOKS

PIGS IN THE PARLOR

9780892280278

A handbook for deliverance from demons and spiritual oppression, patterned after the ministry of Jesus Christ. With over 1 million copies in print worldwide, and translated into more than a dozen languages, *Pigs in the Parlor* remains the authoritative book on the subject of deliverance.

9780892281992

STUDY GUIDE: *PIGS IN THE PARLOR*

Designed as a study tool for either individuals or groups, this guide will enable you to diagnose your personal deliverance needs, walk you through the process of becoming free, and equip you to set others free from demonic torment. Includes questions and answers on a chapter-by-chapter basis as well as new information to further your knowledge of deliverance.

9780892280780

A MANUAL FOR
CHILDREN'S DELIVERANCE

A book to help parents minister to children, and a valuable tool for them to learn how to set their children free from spiritual bondages. Topics include: Jesus' ministry to children, when the womb is unsafe, methods for ministering to children, occult infiltration of childhood, a child's imagination, more.

9780892280179

CONFRONTING FAMILIAR SPIRITS
COUNTERFEITS TO THE HOLY SPIRIT

A person can form a close relationship with an evil spirit, willfully or through ignorance, for the purposes of knowledge or gain. When a person forms a relationship with an evil spirit, he then "has a familiar spirit." Familiar spirits operate as counterfeits to the gifts of the Holy Spirit.

Also Available as an Audio CD
9780892283989 CD

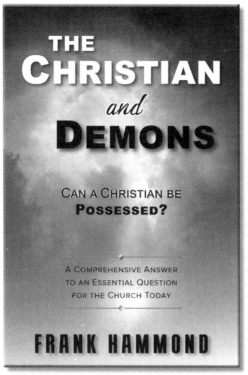

97808922834269

THE CHRISTIAN & DEMONS
CAN A CHRISTIAN BE POSSESSED?

This is one of the most challenging and controversial issues in the Body of Christ today. The uncertainty surrounding this issue creates an obstacle to the greater move of the Holy Spirit taking place on earth. In this concise teaching, Frank Hammond answers the most pressing questions about the deliverance ministry, and whether it applies to Christians today…

- HOW CAN A CHRISTIAN, WITH THE HOLY SPIRIT DWELLING IN HIM OR HER, HAVE A DEMON?

- HOW DOES DEMONIC ACTIVITY COMPARE TO WHAT I HAVE SEEN ON TV OR IN MOVIES?

- ISN'T THIS A MINISTRY FOR REALLY MESSED UP PEOPLE, BEFORE THEY ACCEPT JESUS?

- AREN'T MOST OF MY PROBLEMS PHYSICAL, NOT SPIRITUAL?

- DOES THE BIBLE ACTUALLY SAY CHRISTIANS CAN BE *POSSESSED*?

The Discerning of Spirits

9780892283682

THE DISCERNING OF SPIRITS

BY FRANK HAMMOND

Chief among the spiritual gifts in 1 Corinthians 12 – for the purposes of the ministry of deliverance – is the gift of the *discerning of spirits*. In this booklet, Frank Hammond explains the application of this gift to the believer, and provides examples of how it has worked in his own ministry.

Also Available as an Audio CD

9780892283620 CD

Learn the blessings of Godly Soul-Ties and how to break ungodly Soul-Ties...

"Here at last is a thorough and theologically sound treatment of a little understood subject"
- from the Foreword by **Frank Hammond**

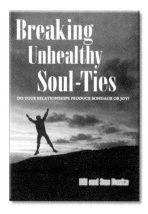

Breaking Unhealthy Soul-Ties
Bill & Sue Banks

Unhealthy soul-ties involve the control of one individual over another, and can be a difficult block to spiritual freedom. Some relationships are healthy and bring blessings into our lives; other types of relationships can bring demonic bondage to our souls. This book assists the reader in diagnosing both healthy and unhealthy relationships, and offers positive steps to personal freedom. **9780892281398**

Study Guide:
Breaking Unhealthy Soul-Ties
Bill & Sue Banks

This Study Guide is a tool that can be used to diagnose and address the soul-ties in your life.

This companion book provides detail into what the soul is, how it functions, and how it can be affected by both positive and negative ties. **9780892282043**

Soul Ties   Frank Hammond

Frank Hammond's booklet on Soul Ties. Good soul ties include marriage, friendship, parent to child, within christians. Bad soul ties include those formed from fornication, evil companions, perverted family ties, with the dead, and demonic ties through the church. **9780892280162**

Audio CD: BY FRANK HAMMOND
Freedom from Demonic Soul Ties (2 CDs)

Frank Hammond teaches on healthy and unhealthy soul ties in this Audio CD, including ministry at the end for breaking demonic soul ties in our lives. **(2 CDs)** **9780892283613 CD**

What Are Obstacles?

9780892282036

OBSTACLES TO DELIVERANCE:

WHY DELIVERANCE SOMETIMES FAILS   FRANK HAMMOND

Why does deliverance sometimes fail? This is, in essence, the same question raised by Jesus' first disciples, when they were unable to cast out a spirit of epilepsy from a young child. Jesus gave a multi-part answer which leads us to take into account the strength of the spirit confronted and the strategy of warfare employed.

Also Available as an Audio CD
9780892283606 CD

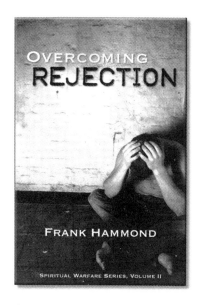

OVERCOMING REJECTION

Frank Hammond addresses the all-too-common root problem of *rejection* and the *fear of rejection* in the lives of believers, and provides steps to be set free. Learn how past experiences can influence our actions, and how we can be made whole. Discover the various causes of rejection, including abuse by parents, peer rejection, marital rejection, Church related rejection, and others.

AUDIO CD:
REJECTION – CAUSE & SOLUTION

In this practical teaching, Frank Hammond highlights the common causes of rejection in our lives, and explains how it can begin as early as in the womb. Frank explains his own battles with rejection which began early in childhood and affected his adult years as a young pastor.

9780892283941 CD

AUDIO CD:
BREAKING DEMONIC STRONGHOLDS

The enemy of our souls has a master plan for each one of us, and it includes the wound of *rejection*. Everyone has to deal with it. The good news is that Jesus provided the overwhelming power to heal our personality — through deliverance, the casting out of demons. This breakthrough teaching by Frank and Ida Mae Hammond was presented in Pigs in the Parlor. Frank Hammond explains demonic strongholds through a common pattern of spirits.

9780892283637 CD

FRANK HAMMOND
ON LIVING AGGRESSIVE SPIRITUAL LIVES

FORGIVING OTHERS: 9780892280766
The Key to Healing & Deliverance

Unforgiveness is an obstacle to our walk with Jesus, and can be a roadblock to the deliverance and freedom of our souls. Frank Hammond explains the spiritual truths regarding the necessity of forgiveness and the blessings of freedom which result.

THE PERILS OF PASSIVITY   9780892281602

There is a purpose in God for each of us - and it is not passivity! Passivity is a foe to all believers in Christ – it can even block deliverance. Deliverance is not a final goal, it is only a sub-goal on the way to fulfill God's purpose in life. Without an aggressive stance against the enemy, we fall back into passivity, and our service to the Lord is hindered. God said to Pharaoh, "Let my people go that they may serve Me" (Exod. 7:16).

THE SAINTS AT WAR   9780892281046

There is a war on for your family, your city and your nation. Christians are in conflict with demons and territorial spirits. This is nothing new... the prophet Daniel confronted the "prince of Persia" when interceding for the captive people of God. Now, learn how you, too, can be involved in fighting for your family, city and nation, and in doing so, change the course of history.

SPIRITUAL WARFARE FOR LOST LOVED ONES

Through spiritual warfare, intercessory prayer, and the ministry of love, we are creating the best possible environment around a loved one to come to know Jesus. Frank Hammond says, "Don't let your family or friends go without resistance. Get in the spiritual battle, fight for your loves ones!"   9780892283842

ON DEFEATING SEXUAL STRONGHOLDS

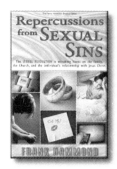

REPERCUSSIONS FROM SEXUAL SINS
FRANK HAMMOND   9780892282050

The sexual revolution has impacted our nation, our church & our family. Promiscuity, nudity, pornography & sexual obscenities are now commonplace. The inevitable consequence of defilement is the loss of fellowship with a holy God. We can break free from the bondage of sexual sin!

THE MARRIAGE BED
FRANK HAMMOND   9780892281862

Can the marriage bed be defiled? Or, does anything and everything go so long as husband and wife are in agreement with their sexual activities? Drawing from God's emphasis on purity and holiness in our lives, this booklet explains how to avoid perverse sexual demonic activity in a home.

MINISTERING TO ABORTION'S AFTERMATH
BILL & SUSAN BANKS   9780892280575

The world has sold us a life without consequences. As a result, millions of women have had abortions. Those who are tormented by pain and regret of this decision have access to the throne of God to receive His mercy and love. They also have access to His mighty delivering power. Read a dozen real-life stories of women who have found deliverance and freedom from the burdens and bondage associated with abortion. Learn how their triumph can be yours!

Frank Hammond
on Breaking Curses in our Lives

The Breaking of Curses   9780892281091

The Bible refers to curses over 230 times, and seventy sins that cause curses are listed in Scripture. Curses are just as real today as they were in Biblical times. Behind every curse there is a demon enacting the curse. Frank Hammond explains what curses are, and how you may deliver yourself and your family from them. Includes generational curses, cursed objects, curses spoken over people, authority–figure curses, witchcraft, and steps to breaking curses.

Audio CD: Spoiling the Enemy's House

Are their obstacles preventing you from succeeding in life? Are there giants in your way, situations that stubbornly refuse to move? Frank Hammond explains the concept of spoiling the enemy's house. He demonstrates the pattern of binding powers and principalities in the supernatural realm, in order to see God's will break through in the natural realm.

9780892284214 CD

Audio CD: Binding the Strongman

There are strongmen in the demonic kingdom, "ruler" spirits over individuals, families, cities and nations. Scripture reveals that there are also Godly, angelic rulers assigned over every family and nation. God has an army. He is the Lord of Hosts, the "Lord of Armies."

9780892283644 CD

Impact Christian Books

Website: WWW.IMPACTCHRISTIANBOOKS.COM

Phone Order Line: (314)-822-3309

Address: IMPACT CHRISTIAN BOOKS
332 Leffingwell Ave. #101
Kirkwood, MO 63122 USA